YOUR KNOWLEDGE HAS

Norman Peitek

Algorithms for Energy Efficient Load Balancing in Cloud Environments

GRIN Publishing

Bibliographic information published by the German National Library:

The German National Library lists this publication in the National Bibliography; detailed bibliographic data are available on the Internet at http://dnb.dnb.de .

Imprint:

Copyright © 2013 GRIN Verlag GmbH
Print and binding: Books on Demand GmbH, Norderstedt Germany
ISBN: 978-3-656-86871-2

This book at GRIN:

http://www.grin.com/en/e-book/286584/algorithms-for-energy-efficient-load-balancing-in-cloud-environments

GRIN - Your knowledge has value

Since its foundation in 1998, GRIN has specialized in publishing academic texts by students, college teachers and other academics as e-book and printed book. The website www.grin.com is an ideal platform for presenting term papers, final papers, scientific essays, dissertations and specialist books.

Visit us on the internet:

http://www.grin.com/

http://www.facebook.com/grincom

http://www.twitter.com/grin_com

Algorithms for Energy Efficient Load Balancing in Cloud Environments

Norman Peitek

Otto-von-Guericke University Magdeburg, Magdeburg, Germany

Abstract. Energy efficiency has a rising importance throughout society. With the growth of large data centers, the energy consumption becomes centralized and nowadays takes a significant amount of the overall electricity consumption of a country. Load balancing algorithms are able to make an existing infrastructure more efficient without major drawbacks. This structured literature research presents the state of the art technology regarding the load balancing approach to make data centers more energy efficient. The state of the art approaches are reviewed for techniques, improvements and consideration of performance effects.

Keywords: energy efficiency, load balancing, cloud computing

1   Introduction

Recent years and the increased awareness of climate change showed the importance of energy efficiency of modern society. Computing is getting more pervasive throughout civilization and consequently is a major factor in the increase of energy demand. Especially with the rise of cloud computing as an idea, large data centers are being built and take a higher and higher percentage of the produced electricity. Recent studies showed that about 2% of the total energy demand of the United States of America is originated from data centers [1]. These host the modern cloud computing environments.

So far the data center research has concentrated on having optimal resource utilization, fast response times, or high availability, but energy efficiency always was of second importance. Modern cloud computing architectures offer a powerful design to fulfill the performance wishes of customers. Since the functional requirements are fulfilled, the data center owner starts to focus on cost reduction. Depending on the source, the costs for energy are between 20% and over 50% of the overall costs. Thus, even a slight decrease in energy consumption has a significant impact on the profitability. Data centers have multiple energy consumers.

1

Minor appliances are lighting or providing energy backup systems. The second largest user is the cooling of the data center [2]. However, the major energy needs are the servers with around 50% of total consumption [2]. Combining that figure with the earlier one, stating that half of the operational costs are energy costs, makes the electricity consumption of the servers responsible for a quarter of all running costs. Additionally, reducing energy consumption of the servers can lead to lower cooling costs. There are multiple approaches to reduce energy consumption in a data center. In order to have a useful result, this search is limited to a specific technique: load balancing.

In order to get a full overview on the topic of energy efficient load balancing algorithms, a structured literature review is conducted. Section 2 introduces how load balancing algorithms can help reducing the energy consumption of a data center. Section 3 describes the process and the different criteria for the search. Section 4 presents the results. Section 5 interprets the results from the previous section. Section 6 summarizes the work in this paper and gives an outlook for the future of optimizing load balancing algorithms towards energy efficiency.

2   Load Balancing in Cloud Environments

Current cloud environments work on virtualized machines (VMs). This requires each heavy-duty physical server to power multiple VMs at the same time. The VMs can have different configurations and service level agreements (SLAs) depending on the customer. Mainly, three abilities make it possible to save energy:

- overallocation,
- live migration,
- shutting down servers, depending on the overall data center load.

Overallocation is the transfer of the overbooking principle, commonly practiced in the hotel and airline industry, to the IT industry [3]. In the data center context it means that the placed VMs on the physical server have more resources reserved than the server actually has available. For example, the server has 24 GB of RAM and three VMs with 12 GB of RAM configuration are currently running on this machine. This is only possible as long as the VMs do not need their full RAM capacity, since the server only has 24 GB and not the required 36 GB. However, the load for one or multiple VMs could change at any time and increase the RAM demand. The data center owner wants to avoid a potentially costly SLA violation. Thus, one of the VMs should run on a different server.

Live migration is a technique to move an active VM from one server to another without an interruption in the availability or the ongoing computing. Nevertheless, live migration is expensive. During the time beginning with the transfer until the end of the transfer, both physical machines reserve the full VM capacity. Additionally, it causes traffic on the data center internal network, which is often the scarcest entity, and the data center storage area network as well.

The situation in a cloud environment is that of hundreds of physical machines powering thousands of VMs with different configurations and SLAs, and quickly changing loads. Load balancing algorithms place and live migrate VMs on the controlled amount of running servers. This field has been researched with different optimization goals (up time, response time, minimizing internal traffic). As shown in the introduction, the optimization towards energy efficiency has a direct impact on the costs of the data center, which makes this goal attractive.

3 Search Strategy and Review Protocol

A literature review is supposed to be reproducible. Thus, the following subchapters describe different aspects of the paper search, selection, and refinement.

3.1 Research Goals

RQ1: What techniques are used by load balancing algorithms to increase energy efficiency?

Load balancing is not a new problem. A very similar field was researched during the time of distributed computing in the 1950's. Exactly as in the past, there are different ideas to balance the load in a cloud environment. This research question aims to grasp the basic concept behind the algorithm. An overview of the different techniques gives a good opportunity to understand what popular approaches are, where the research is going, and what could come in the future.

RQ2: How are the energy efficiency improvements measured?

The researcher who has an idea to improve energy efficiency needs to prove his advancement in a way. This could be, for example, an experiment within his data center or a simulation with real load data. However, if he proves his advancement with an experiment within his own data center, the idea is valid for one particular case. That does not necessarily mean that it will work as well for any other data center with largely different setups. In other words, thinking about how the researcher showed his improvement, gives a hint about the generality of his solution. A slightly higher efficiency in all cases is preferable to a largely higher efficiency in one case which rarely occurs. Also, looking into this question shows the limitations of the algorithms, i.e. if it is only applicable for low-load situations. These points make this an important research question.

RQ3: Does applying the algorithm in order to reduce energy consumption affect overall performance or system reliability?

The concept of load balancing seems to be an advantage without a drawback. The algorithms can reduce energy consumption with simultaneously no performance drops. However, real world experiments indicate that it does have a drawback and it does affect the system. This question is additional to the actual literature research and does not limit the search for different algorithms. Nevertheless, in order to get an idea out of the research lab into a running data center, the research must consider downsides too. A data center owner who saves money on energy but i.e. loses three times as much in revenue will not think the algorithm is effective. This questions aims to clarify if and how many of the current researchers pay attention to this matter.

3.2 Search Term

The search term is the following expression:

```
energy efficiency OR energy reduction OR reduce consumption OR energy aware OR
                energy saving OR green IT or energy costs
                              AND
load balancing OR load distribution OR vm migration OR consolidation algorithm OR
  resource management OR virtual machines OR allocation OR scheduling OR capacity
                           management
                              AND
        cloud computing OR data center OR cluster computing systems
                          SINCE 2008
```

In order to get the best search results, the search term was split into three parts which are combined with an AND operator. The first part includes synonyms for energy efficiency or reducing energy consumption. The second part includes synonyms for load balancing. This is necessary since there are multiple approaches to reduce energy consumption, but this literature review is only focused on load balancing techniques. The last part limits the search to cloud environments. Unfortunately, not every researcher likes the term "cloud computing", so "data center" and "cluster computing systems" were added. Cluster computing meant something related but slightly different in the past. In order to specify that cluster computing means cloud computing, no paper before 2008 is accepted. The year 2008 was the year in which the term cloud computing started to occur in the research of computer science.

3.3 Source Databases

This search term is used to find all relevant publications in this particular matter. Table 1 shows the searched databases and the result figures.

Database	ACM Digital Library	IEEE Xplore Digital Library
Results	94	266
1. Refinement	5	21
2. Refinement	1	7

Table 1. Searched Databases and Results

IBM Technical Papers, Lecture Notes in Computer Science, and Lecture Notes in Control and Information Sciences were consulted, but did not return any results. Google Scholar was not included, since the search term input is very limited and it did not offer an efficient way to discover papers in this very specific research field.

3.4 Selection and Refinement Process

The search query returned 360 results. These results were tested against the first refinement criteria, which are described in Table 2. It reduced the publications which were sufficient for this literature research to 28. All of the articles were reviewed in regards to the research questions and included into the results.

Inclusion criteria	Exclusion criteria
The setting is a cloud computing environment (or similarly worded)	The publication requires precise hardware configurations
The publication describes specifically a technique to reduce energy consumption within one data center	The publication does not have an emphasis on energy efficiency
The publication is in English	

Table 2. Inclusion and Exclusion Criteria for First Refinement

While the criteria for the first refinement are sufficient for an overview of the techniques and could potentially answer RQ1 and RQ2, the articles may not answer RQ3. In order to have a useful selection of literature to evaluate the last research question, a second refinement on the basis of the results of the first refinement is performed. The criteria are stated in Table 3.

Inclusion criteria	Exclusion criteria
The publication considers the algorithm's effect on performance	The publication does not clearly describe the evaluation of the results

Table 3. Inclusion and Exclusion Criteria for Second Refinement

4 Results

4.1 First Refinement

Technique	# of Publications	rounded in %	Publications
Static (tresholds, rule-based)	8	30%	[4], [5], [6], [7], [8], [9], [10], [11]
Load Prediction	6	23%	[12], [13], [5], [14], [15], [16]
Dynamic Programming	3	12%	[17], [18], [19]
Multi-objective	3	12%	[20], [21], [22]
Genetic Programming	3	12%	[13], [20], [23]
Linear Programming	2	8%	[12], [24]
Others (only one appearance per approach)	5	19%	Constraint Programming [25], Reinforced Learning [26], Optimized Live Migration [27], Optimized Network [28], Fuzzy Cost Function [29]

Table 4. Results grouped after the used technique

Note: The overall percentage exceeds 100% due to rounding errors and a few papers appear more than once, i.e. [20] is multi-objective and predicts the future load.

4.2 Second Refinement

Performance evaluation	# of Publications	rounded in % (out of 26 total)	Publications
SLA Violations measured	4	15%	[4], [6], [7], [14]
SLA Violation Cost-awareness	3	12%	[20], [21], [22]
Performance drop measured	1	4%	[19]

5 Discussion

5.1 RQ1

The majority of the found publications improve the bin-packing-problem of the load balancing. In other words, they implement a better algorithm to decide which VM should be placed on what PM. While early works in 2010 for example use simple thresholds [4], the methods get more complex over time. The optimization problem is tackled with the already existing ideas of optimization theory from other fields of science, like mathematics or economics. Dynamic programming with three papers, linear programming, and genetic algorithms with each two publications are the most common implementations.

The mandatory of the published papers are applying a reactive algorithm. This means that they act as soon as a threshold is exceeded, but do not proactively prevent such a situation. Predicting the future workload is a powerful tool, which helps to use overallocation while simultaneously not decreasing the service level. Thus, scientists implemented predictors to tackle this insufficiency. While the results are consistently successful, the predictor method varies between quadratic exponential smoothing [13], linear prediction [5], neural network prediction [14], and a predictive Bayesian network [15].

Only two publications use a different method besides improving load balancing or predicting future workloads. One group of scientists improved the live migration tool to increase energy efficiency [27]. The other group decreased energy consumption by optimizing the load balancing towards network awareness and thus being able to turn off network switches [28].

Aiming for high resource utilization is a very similar problem to the energy efficiency increase attempts in the topic of data center optimization. It is notable that my results did not include any research which attempted to build a decentralized algorithm. In the past, while optimizing for resource utilization instead of energy efficiency, decentralized approaches were tested [30].

5.2 RQ2

All of the publications in the result use a simulation as the proof. It is remarkable that none use an analytical or experimental process. Nevertheless, it is not surprising considering the complexity of the problem. An analytical proof is too complex and an experiment in a real-world data center too riskful and too interrupting for the running operation.

The distinction, however, is between the quality of the simulations. Only a few authors use real data for their simulations, i.e. [13] or [18]. Additionally, most of the papers after the first refinement only test against one specific workload. That proves the effectiveness for this particular situation, but does not deliver a specific statement about the effectiveness in general.

5.3 RQ3

As expected, the number of authors who directly consider and test for performance effects is low. However, especially the multi-objective frameworks do include the service level agreements and their violation costs, i.e [21] or [22]. Thus, the literature research discovered that this important question is still ambiguous, but less urgent since the modern algorithms rather have higher energy consumption than causing SLA violation costs. Specific papers for performance issues are becoming available [31].

5.4   Current Status of the Research

Research Attention

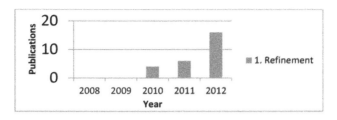

Table 5. Published Paper per Year after First Refinement

Table 5 illustrates the publications per year after the first refinement was completed. It clearly shows a huge growth every year. The growing research attention hints towards a high importance of energy efficient data centers. Additionally, the high number of publications indicates that this topic is interesting for the scientific community and still has unanswered questions.

Open questions and insufficiencies

This literature review discovered a few weaknesses with today's research. Firstly, many papers only consider low-load situations. In a cloud environment it is unlikely, since higher utilization is one of the main advantages. Of course, a low-load situation offers much higher energy savings, but it does not state the powerfulness in real world situations. Secondly, most of the papers do not consider performance interferences [32], which prevents the algorithm from being transferred to a real world use. Thirdly, it is questionable that many simulations assume the same kind of infrastructure for the whole data center. In practice, it is unlikely that the data center is running on the exact same configuration for all physical machines.

Most of the literature uses a simulation as proof of improved energy efficiency. However, potential secondary effects are not included in these results. If the algorithms shut down a whole rack of servers, the overall heat creation could be reduced. Thus, reducing the necessary cooling and further improving overall energy efficiency.

5.5 Load Balancing Algorithm Architecture

After reviewing the past and current research publications, it is possible to create a general design template for load balancing algorithms.

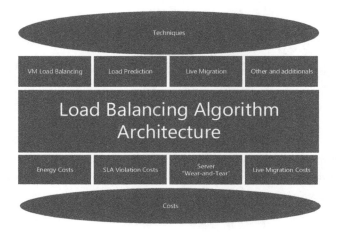

Fig. 1. Load Balancing Algorithm Architecture

The optimal design is complex and multi-objective towards the costs and techniques. This means the design is flexible enough to be extended by additional objectives or additional techniques [25].

For example on the objective side, the decision making process of the load balance optimization is based on a cost function. The cost function includes the costs of energy, SLA violation, the wear-and-tear of physical machines by regularly turning them on and off, and the live migration costs. A good approach would be able to add further customized costs of the data center, i.e. the most important customer should be satisfied (in other words, SLA violations with that customer are more expansive than the actual contract states). Recent publications are coming closer to that goal [21].

6 Limitations

The search reflected on papers from only two sources. This potentially limits the completeness of this state of the art overview. However, the search in other science databases for this very specific topic was unsuccessful. Considering this, adding sources from not scientifically reviewed sources, like Microsoft Research [33], could give insights on new innovative ideas.

Furthermore, this literature review only considered load balancing algorithms. Further actions towards lower energy consumption could be adding hardware-based energy savers (DVFS [34], memory [35]) or reducing the required cooling [34, 36]. The optimal configuration for a data center is likely to be an optimization with multiple approaches. Additionally, if applicable, an optimization over multiple data centers is possible as well [37].

7   Conclusion and Further Work

The advantage of the presented algorithms is the independency to the technical occurrence of the data center. The system can be based on different hardware and have no information about the cooling status, and the load balancing algorithms will still reach their goals. Unlike the other possible approaches (DVFS, partial memory shutdown) to save energy, the load balancing algorithms have an aspect of generality. Data centers are very diverse and this universal method makes the idea practical. The likelihood of getting one of the algorithms out of the lab and actually running in a large data center makes this research so attractive.

The topic of energy efficient load balancing algorithms is under heavy research at the moment and still receives increasing attention, even though there seems to be a limit in effectiveness [38]. The research progress advanced significantly in the last years. There are still questions about the load balancing and the effects around it. So far the different aspects and techniques of load balancing were researched. It is time to combine the research to build a fully-functional prototype, implementing the full architecture and not just elements [39]. This will be researched in the future while large data centers and the demand for energy efficient load balancing are still growing.

References

[1] Jonathan Koomey, *Growth in Data center electricity use 2005 to 2010.*

[2] Emerson Network Power, *Five Strategies for Cutting Data Center Energy Costs Through Enhanced Cooling Efficiency.*

[3] A. Sulistio, K. H. Kim, and R. Buyya, "Managing Cancellations and No-Shows of Reservations with Overbooking to Increase Resource Revenue," in *Proceedings of the 2008 Eighth IEEE International Symposium on Cluster Computing and the Grid*: IEEE Computer Society, 2008, pp. 267–276.

[4] A. Beloglazov and R. Buyya, "Adaptive threshold-based approach for energy-efficient consolidation of virtual machines in cloud data centers," in *Proceedings of the 8th International Workshop on Middleware for Grids, Clouds and e-Science*, New York, NY, USA: ACM, 2010, pp. 4:1-4:6.

[5] B. Guenter, N. Jain, and C. Williams, Eds, *Managing cost, performance, and reliability tradeoffs for energy-aware server provisioning.* INFOCOM, Proceedings IEEE, 2011.

[6] M. Guazzone, C. Anglano, and M. Canonico, Eds, *Energy-Efficient Resource Management for Cloud Computing Infrastructures.* Cloud Computing Technology and Science (CloudCom), 2011 IEEE Third International Conference on, 2011.

[7] M.M. Taheri and K. Zamanifar, Eds, *2-phase optimization method for energy aware scheduling of virtual machines in cloud data centers.* Internet Technology and Secured Transactions (ICITST), 2011 International Conference for, 2011.

[8] Wang Xiaoli and Liu Zhanghui, Eds, *An Energy-Aware VMs Placement Algorithm in Cloud Computing Environment.* Intelligent System Design and Engineering Application (ISDEA), 2012 Second International Conference on, 2012.

[9] R. Karthikeyan and P. Chitra, Eds, *Novel heuristics energy efficiency approach for cloud data center.* Advanced Communication Control and Computing Technologies (ICACCCT), 2012 IEEE International Conference on, 2012.

[10] C. Kleineweber, A. Keller, O. Niehorster, and A. Brinkmann, Eds, *Rule-Based Mapping of Virtual Machines in Clouds.* Parallel, Distributed and Network-Based Processing (PDP), 2011 19th Euromicro International Conference on, 2011.

[11] D. Borgetto, M. Maurer, G. Da-Costa, J. Pierson, and I. Brandic, Eds, *Energy-efficient and SLA-aware management of IaaS clouds.* Future Energy Systems: Where Energy, Computing and Communication Meet (e-Energy), 2012 Third International Conference on, 2012.

[12] B. Kantarci and H. T. Mouftah, "Optimal Reconfiguration of the Cloud Network for Maximum Energy Savings," in *Proceedings of the 2012 12th IEEE/ACM International Symposium on Cluster, Cloud and Grid Computing (ccgrid 2012)*, Washington, DC, USA: IEEE Computer Society, 2012, pp. 835–840.

[13] Haibo Mi, Huaimin Wang, Gang Yin, Yangfan Zhou, Dianxi Shi, and Lin Yuan, Eds, *Online Self-Reconfiguration with Performance Guarantee for Energy-Efficient Large-Scale Cloud Computing Data Centers*. Services Computing (SCC), 2010 IEEE International Conference on, 2010.

[14] I.S. Moreno and Jie Xu, Eds, *Neural Network-Based Overallocation for Improved Energy-Efficiency in Real-Time Cloud Environments*. Object/Component/Service-Oriented Real-Time Distributed Computing (ISORC), IEEE 15th International Symposium on, 2012.

[15] Jian Li, Kai Shuang, Sen Su, Qingjia Huang, Peng Xu, Xiang Cheng, and Jie Wang, Eds, *Reducing Operational Costs through Consolidation with Resource Prediction in the Cloud*. Cluster, Cloud and Grid Computing (CCGrid), 2012 12th IEEE/ACM International Symposium on, 2012.

[16] I.S. Moreno and Jie Xu, Eds, *Customer-aware resource overallocation to improve energy efficiency in realtime Cloud Computing data centers*. Service-Oriented Computing and Applications (SOCA), 2011 IEEE International Conference on, 2011.

[17] H. Goudarzi, M. Ghasemazar, and M. Pedram, "SLA-based Optimization of Power and Migration Cost in Cloud Computing," in *Proceedings of the 2012 12th IEEE/ACM International Symposium on Cluster, Cloud and Grid Computing (ccgrid 2012)*, Washington, DC, USA: IEEE Computer Society, 2012, pp. 172–179.

[18] V. Mathew, R.K. Sitaraman, and P. Shenoy, Eds, *Energy-aware load balancing in content delivery networks*. INFOCOM, 2012 Proceedings IEEE, 2012.

[19] H. Goudarzi and M. Pedram, Eds, *Energy-Efficient Virtual Machine Replication and Placement in a Cloud Computing System*. Cloud Computing (CLOUD), 2012 IEEE 5th International Conference on, 2012.

[20] Li Xu, Zhibin Zeng, and Xiucai Ye, Eds, *Multi-objective Optimization Based Virtual Resource Allocation Strategy for Cloud Computing*. Computer and Information Science (ICIS), 2012 IEEE/ACIS 11th International Conference on, 2012.

[21] Bo Yin and Lin Lin, Eds, *Energy reducing dynamic multi-dimensional resource allocation in cloud data center*. Network Operations and Management Symposium (APNOMS), 2012 14th Asia-Pacific, 2012.

15

[22] Wei Deng, Fangming Liu, Hai Jin, Xiaofei Liao, Haikun Liu, and Li Chen, Eds, *Lifetime or energy: Consolidating servers with reliability control in virtualized cloud datacenters*. Cloud Computing Technology and Science (CloudCom), 2012 IEEE 4th International Conference on, 2012.

[23] Gaojin Wen, Shengzhong Feng, Yanyi Wan, Pingchuang Jiang, and Senlin Zhang, Eds, *Energy-aware application scheduling based on genetic algorithm*. Natural Computation (ICNC), 2011 Seventh International Conference on, 2011.

[24] Yongqiang Gao, Zhengwei Qi, Yubin Wu, Rui Wang, Liang Liu, Jitao Xu, and Haibing Guan, Eds, *A Power and Performance Management Framework for Virtualized Server Clusters*. Green Computing and Communications (GreenCom), 2011 IEEE/ACM International Conference on, 2011.

[25] C. Dupont, T. Schulze, G. Giuliani, A. Somov, and F. Hermenier, "An energy aware framework for virtual machine placement in cloud federated data centres," in *Proceedings of the 3rd International Conference on Future Energy Systems: Where Energy, Computing and Communication Meet*, New York, NY, USA: ACM, 2012, pp. 4:1-4:10.

[26] Jingling Yuan, Xing Jiang, Luo Zhong, and Hui Yu, Eds, *Energy Aware Resource Scheduling Algorithm for Data Center Using Reinforcement Learning*. Intelligent Computation Technology and Automation (ICICTA), 2012 Fifth International Conference on, 2012.

[27] Bing Wei, Chuang Lin, and Xiangzhen Kong, Eds, *Energy optimized modeling for live migration in virtual data center*. Computer Science and Network Technology (ICCSNT), 2011 International Conference on, 2011.

[28] H. Shirayanagi, H. Yamada, and K. Kono, Eds, *Honeyguide: A VM migration-aware network topology for saving energy consumption in data center networks*. Computers and Communications (ISCC), 2012 IEEE Symposium on, 2012.

[29] R. Yamini, Ed, *Power management in cloud computing using green algorithm*. Advances in Engineering, Science and Management (ICAESM), International Conference on, 2012.

[30] A. Quiroz, Hyunjoo Kim, M. Parashar, N. Gnanasambandam, and N. Sharma, Eds, *Towards autonomic workload provisioning for enterprise Grids and clouds*. Grid Computing, 2009 10th IEEE/ACM International Conference on, 2009.

[31] Truong Vinh Truong Duy, Y. Sato, and Y. Inoguchi, Eds, *Performance evaluation of a Green Scheduling Algorithm for energy savings in Cloud computing*. Parallel & Dis-

tributed Processing, Workshops and Phd Forum (IPDPSW), 2010 IEEE International Symposium on, 2010.

[32] I.S. Moreno, R. Yang, J. Xu, and T. Wo, Eds, *Improved energy-efficiency in cloud datacenters with interference-aware virtual machine placement.* Autonomous Decentralized Systems (ISADS), 2013 IEEE Eleventh International Symposium on, 2013.

[33] Microsoft Research, *Energy-Efficient Enterprise and Cloud Computing.* Available: http://research.microsoft.com/en-us/projects/eec/.

[34] Lago, Daniel Guimaraes do, Madeira, Edmundo R. M, and L. F. Bittencourt, "Power-aware virtual machine scheduling on clouds using active cooling control and DVFS," in *Proceedings of the 9th International Workshop on Middleware for Grids, Clouds and e-Science*, New York, NY, USA: ACM, 2011, pp. 2:1-2:6.

[35] K. Sudan, S. Srinivasan, R. Balasubramanian, and R. Iyer, "Optimizing datacenter power with memory system levers for guaranteed quality-of-service," in *Proceedings of the 21st international conference on Parallel architectures and compilation techniques*, New York, NY, USA: ACM, 2012, pp. 117–126.

[36] Hui Chen, Meina Song, Junde Song, A. Gavrilovska, and K. Schwan, Eds, *HEaRS: A Hierarchical Energy-Aware Resource Scheduler for Virtualized Data Centers.* Cluster Computing (CLUSTER), 2011 IEEE International Conference on, 2011.

[37] V.D. Justafort and S. Pierre, Eds, *Performance-aware virtual machine allocation approach in an intercloud environment.* Electrical & Computer Engineering (CCECE), 2012 25th IEEE Canadian Conference on, 2012.

[38] X. Leon and L. Navarro, Eds, *Limits of energy saving for the allocation of data center resources to networked applications.* INFOCOM, 2011 Proceedings IEEE, 2011.

[39] E. Feller, C. Rohr, D. Margery, and C. Morin, Eds, *Energy Management in IaaS Clouds: A Holistic Approach.* Cloud Computing (CLOUD), IEEE 5th International Conference on, 2012.